Poems of Love and Loss

Lessons Learned

Bonnie Shetters Wise

ISBN: 979-8-89122-293-9

Dedication

This book of Poems is dedicated to Isaac Matthew Wise, Jr. (Jackie), my husband, from June 7, 1963, to May 1, 2012.

I began writing a thought or a sentence after Jackie passed away, something like I miss you today or I visited your grave today, and later when I looked back at them, I would turn them into a poem. Each one is special and means more to me than just a few words on paper. I was blessed beyond measure to have a love so strong and true. These words come easily from my heart because it is still full of love for him, even after all these years.

Acknowledgment

I would like to thank my Family and Friends for their encouragement and support. My G.I.R.L.S. for always being here for me, and who have encouraged me to write this book of poems.

Thank you especially to the team at Amazon Publishing for their time and patience with me as I add, change, and try to complete this book. Especially to the following:

- Robinson Germaine
- Ashley Clements
- Adam Willems

Table of Contents

About the Author

I have had the privilege of being a friend of Bonnie Shetters Wise for many years. I have watched her through hardships and trials, as well as joyous times. She has remained constantly steadfast, no matter the situation.

Bonnie is a multi-talented lady, full of love and laughter, even in the worst of times. I've watched her work two jobs, sometimes three at a time, all the while keeping her home and kids in order. She and her husband, Jackie, shared a love that has even surpassed his passing.

Her first book, ONE DAY AT A TIME, is a day-by-day journal of that love. Her poems, stories, and writings will be a delight to all who read.

Read carefully, you just might find yourself in her writings.

– Ginger Montgomery

61 years ago, on June 7, 1963, we began a journey that was one of many surprises, heartaches, good times, bad times, but most of all, a time of growing old together and learning the meaning of love and commitment. There are many things I wish I could go back and do differently – not major things. Little things like sitting outside and listening to the rain with him or just slowing down and taking the time to talk more.

One thing I wish I could share today and help someone is to show you that there is not always tomorrow. Angry words said today may be the last words you speak to each other. That little peck on the cheek may be the last kiss you get. The I love you that you whisper as you're running out the door may be the last time you have the opportunity to say it. Tomorrow is not guaranteed, so make the most of today; don't take anyone or anything for granted.

I was fortunate that I didn't lose him suddenly; we had almost 9 months after his surgery, but that didn't make it any easier. I spent every day with him, and we talked, laughed, and cried. I tried so hard to make him well and he tried just as hard to do everything, but it wasn't meant to be. His heart was just too weak.

You never know when your time on earth will be done, so make the most of every day. Don't let anything come between you and those you love. There is nothing worth the love of your family, so don't let pride stand in your way. If there is someone who owes you an apology, be the bigger person and make it your priority to get things straightened out. Life is too short!

Jackie and I didn't have a perfect or easy life, but we did love each other, and we both knew it. He loved me so much that with his last breath, he looked at me and said please. I loved him enough that I said OK, and he closed his eyes.

We didn't know 61 years ago how all this would turn out. Would I go back and do it again? Yes, in a minute. I had the love of my life with me, and I never had to worry or wonder if he loved me. I knew it, and he knew I felt the same way about him.

I miss him as much today as I did the day he left, and it is just as lonely. My heart broke the day he died, and it still hurts. I work, I go places and I spend time with my family because life does go on. I have a happy life and loving family and friends, but even in a crowd of people, I miss that one who always held my hand and gave me a smile or a big hug.

The 1963 Tigers are the best!

We have passed our many tests.

We stay in touch and spend time together,

Bonds from then have never been severed.

I walked outside this morning!

I walked outside this morning to watch the sunrise.

It was amazing to me, and much to my surprise:

The sky was blue, the clouds were white,

And peeping through, was a bright light.

May be an image of tree, eclipse, twilight and cloud

The clouds opened, and the sun came through-

Framed with a backdrop of a beautiful blue hue.

Thank you, God, for a beautiful sunrise.

A beautiful day you have supplied. Never take for granted a
beautiful scene.

God has placed this beauty in everything.

In a flower that blooms or a cloud in the sky.

Look at the colors of a butterfly.

All these things God gave us to enjoy.

Take the time to slow down to enjoy them more.

The days come slowly but fly by fast.

Make memories today, they will always last.

Live a Life Strong and True

Today my mind was wondering…
To days gone by and passed.
How God leads and guides us
To His chosen path.

A day goes by so quickly,
But don't give up the fight.
Live your life and keep it bright.
Shining your love like a beam of light.

A bright light with a soft glow…
Who you help, you may never know!
Your smile may brighten the way,
For some lost soul out there today.

Live a life, so strong and true.
That others know they can depend on you…
Set an example of truth and love.
Pointing all others to God above.

In Sickness and In Health

We face many things in sickness and in health,
And never found that fountain of wealth.
Love needs no money, just faith and trust.
We had that; it was a must.

Your sickness only made us closer,
All through the years.
Our three children were a gift from God.
We trusted Him, whatever our lot.

Grandchildren and greats were next in line,
No better children could we ever find.
Our love continued and became even stronger,
It helped you to fight cancer and live even longer.

Death did come and will come to us all.
You were always so brave, just standing tall.

I miss you so much, I always will.

No one your place can ever fill.

I love you then, I love you now.

You're in heaven with never a frown.

We will all see you soon,

Look for us just past the moon.

The Day You Left

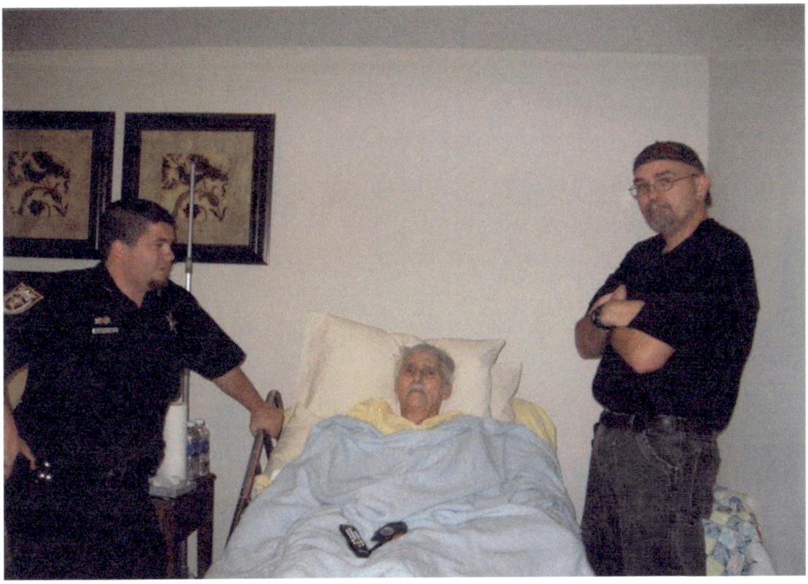

By your side, I held your hand.
Looked into your eyes, my handsome man.
You looked at me and I saw your smile.
The angels were there, right by your side.

Yes, in your face, I saw the pain.
I knew you would never be the same.
You looked at me and I saw you smile?
The angels were there right by your side.

You squeeze my hand, a tender touch!
How could we love each other so much?
God gave me you, and now it was time…
To give you back, to take away your pain.

My earthly loss was heaven's gain.

Missing You

Sitting here today and missing you…
Just lonely, not sad or blue.
I miss you coming home after a long day at work,
Just driving along in your big green Hess truck.

A true love and a happy marriage,
Ended by cancer, a terrible savage.
I miss you today, and I always will!
No one your place can ever fill.

A million memories of days gone by,
When you and I were always side-by-side.
So goodbye, for now, I love you dearly,
Until in heaven, I'll see you more clearly.

I Am Blessed

I have been blessed in my life,
But it has not come without heartache and strife.
We work together, Jackie and I…
Always a couple and always a smile

Times were hard when sickness came,
Encephalitis left, but he was never the same.
He was left weak and terribly thin,
Never to be completely healthy again.

Heart attacks came, one by one,
A fall from a truck and his back was done.
A rotator cuff, back surgery twice.
Once through the stomach and once in the back.

Neck surgery, open heart surgery all followed, too.
Soon there was no work that he could do.
I had two jobs, finally three…
But that was OK, I was blessed with these.

God gave me the strength to carry on,
He kept me well, happy and strong.
One Day at a Time became our song.
I knew now that he would never get strong.

Jackie fought a good fight; he was faithful and true.
He never failed to say I love you!
Cancer came and surgery followed.
A nicked artery in his throat left him, unable to swallow.

When God took him home, I held his hand.
His eyes met mine as he whispered, "Please."
I knew he was asking me to let him leave.
OK, I whispered with a broken heart.

His eyes closed; his body relaxed,
He was home now and would not be back.

Letter to Heaven

I visited your grave today to clean to talk.

I wish that I could hold your hand and take a little walk.

I would say how much I love you, but I know where you are.

Every time I look up to heaven, I see your shining star!

God took you home, and in heaven, you remain,
But the lives you touched here will never be the same.
You were an example of true love, kindness, and forgiveness.
A man who loved his family and always put them first.

I wish I had known that they would be your last
The time had gone by, just way too fast!
You looked at me, and as your eyes met mine,
I knew right then, it was in God's time.

You said please, I said OK.
Your eyes closed; your body relaxed.
I knew you had left and you would not be back.
You were home, your pain was gone.
We were left here to carry on.

My heart is in a million pieces, the heartache is real.
There's no adequate way to describe the pain I always feel.
I wish that I could see you, to hold your hand once more.
To hear you say again that I am the only one that you love and adore.

Until the day, I'll leave this earth, you're the only love, I know!

I see you in the faces of our children, the ones we hold so dear.
Your grandchildren and the greats, too…
I just wish they all had the opportunity to meet you.

Well, I cleaned the dust away today and visited for a while.
I truly hope our talk brought you a big, happy smile.
I swear, I heard you say "Dollbaby" as the wind blew through the trees.
I knew right then and there, you will always be here to watch over me.

Love and miss you today!

Thinking about You

Eleven years ago, God took you home.
It's not always easy being alone.
I loved you from the day we met,
Our love was strong, I'll never forget.

You were such a quiet, handsome man,
A love like hours was hard to understand.
Our vows, never broken…
Our words, I love you, are often spoken.

Your time on earth came to an end,
But I will always love you, my husband, my friend.
I will see you again when God calls me home,
My love for you will always be strong.

I love you, always and forever.
Forget you, no, not ever.
Until the day I die…
You will always be right by my side.

I Held You In My Arms Last Night

Your arms held me tight,

And we danced all through the night.

We were young, so happy and free.

Our love was there, easy to see.

The years passed by, quickly they flew.
We were happy and never blue!
Our children came and so quickly they grew.
Then, just like that, it was just me and you!

Time changes everything, just like they say.
So well I remember that faithful day.
Cancer came, and you were racked with pain.
Your health, you could never regain.

God called you home, your pain was gone.
I was left here, all alone.
So yes, I held you in my arms last night…
It was only a dream, but it felt right.

I Will Forever Love Only You

What can I say? What can I do?

I will forever love only you!

Cancer came and you had to leave.

My heart will forever grieve.

Life goes on, our children's families are now grown.

Great grands are now all at home.

Eight grand and eight greats,

I wish you were here to celebrate.

I can't bring you back, nor do I wish to do so.

God said it was time for you to go.

We love you; we miss you, but we understand.

You had to go when He took your hand.

When the sun shines bright, we know it's you.

Smiling on us so we won't be blue.

Keep smiling on us as we wait for our time.

God knows what is best on down the line.

For My Sister

My sister passed away, and I was driving home alone from her funeral. I turned off I-95 to exit onto Highway 17 and I stopped at the stop sign, and straight in front of me, there was A forest of trees. Clouds above the trees allowed the sun to peak through them with a beautiful bright light. Without even thinking, I said thank you, God, for letting me know Dean was there.

It was as if God knew I needed Him to let me know she was home and happy. When I got home, these are the words I wrote from my heart.

The sun was still shining bright.
It was almost time to go down for the night.
God knew we needed to see the glow from my sister,
With a voice that was only a soft whisper.

I'm here, I'm safe and all is well.
It's beautiful and so much more than I can tell.
The bells ring, the angels sing.
There's beauty and harmony in everything.

Don't be sad, don't miss me!
I will be here, and you will see.
The best of everything is waiting for you.
So, smile, don't cry, and don't be blue.

When God calls you and it's time to go,
You will leave here with a heavenly glow.
Life is short on earth, but forever in heaven.
I'll see you all soon, yes, all of us, all 11.

James, Terri, Caleb, and many others,

Mom and Dad, three sisters and four brothers!

We're together, waiting for you!

Trust in God, and don't be blue!

See you all soon!

Written for my sister, Dean Tyre

Bonnie Sue Wise

5/30/23

Family Reunion two weeks before Dean passed away. God knew we needed to all be together one more time before she left us. I'm so thankful that He placed this reunion on my heart and most of us were there. We never know when it may be the last time that we will see those we love.

The Visiting Cardinal

It has been said that the Cardinals are a sign of hope and a reminder that tough times will not last forever.

A bird with feathers, so bright and red,
Stopped by today in my flower bed.
A message from you, I knew you'd find a way.
I only wish you could have stayed.

God had sent the red bird from up above,
To remind me of his amazing grace and love.
A message of love to remind me of you,
Forever, honest, and always true.

God is love, and love remains.
But since you left, our lives have changed.
You left a place no one can fill.
Our love for you, is still very real.

We'll see you again, one happy day,
But until then, this is where we stay.
I will look for you with every smile.
And go until I walk my last mile!

A Red Bird

A red bird came to visit me today.
He perched in a tree nearby.
I felt him watching me as I glanced into his eyes.
I saw a message that God had sent,
A message of love, hope, and faith.

Hang in there, and don't give up.
My love and faith will keep you going.
Where there is hope, there is love,
We are blessed by God above.

So, in your day, if a cardinal is near,
Remember, love, life, faith, and have no fear.
You're in Heaven, but I feel you here.

I'm glad you came by today,
You're always near me when I pray,
And I realize that you can't stay –
I know you are never far away.

A red bird came to comfort me…

Until again, your face, I see.

Christmas Is Coming

Christmas is coming, but it won't be the same.
My Earthly loss was Heaven's gain.
Our years together were always the best,
Your body grew tired, and God took you to rest.

Christmas is a time to celebrate.
Our years together were always great.
We went through pain, sorrow, sickness, and death.
Our love never failed, no matter the test.

Seasons have come, and seasons have gone,
My love for you is still just as strong.
I can't let go; my loss is so great.
There aren't many days that my heart doesn't ache.

Life does go on, and all is well.
The children, grandchildren, and greats never fail.
They remember Papa Jack and the stories he could tell.
You can rest easy in heaven, knowing all is well.

I'll see you again, one day soon, I know,
As God's plan for me continues to grow.
Our time on Earth is limited, we all know.
It won't be long before to Heaven we will go.

Valentines Day

I wrote this today, not because I'm sad or lonely but as a reminder to everyone.... don't take anything for granted. You never know what a day will bring, and I try to remember our days together. Valentine's Day didn't mean that I would get a gift or flowers, it was even better. I always had a hug, a kiss, and "A Happy Valentine's Day, Sweetheart." (I did occasionally get gifts, but that wasn't the important part.)

I miss you more with every passing hour.

From June 7, 1963, to May 1, 2012.

We still heard our wedding bells.
Our love stood the test of time,
shared by both, our stars were aligned.
So, I'm celebrating our love alone today,
because you had to go away.

Cancer came, and you had to leave,
But I know I should not grieve.
I'll see you again, I just don't know when.
So, happy Valentine's Day until I do,
Rest easy, Sweetheart, I will always love only you.

Missing my Valentine today, I would love to have just a few minutes, or even one… But here is something for you today that I learned from Jackie.

It's not the cards, flowers or a present, it's the fact that you want to show them your love. Every day with your loved one should be treated as a remarkable one and leave an impression.

It has been 5 years, 9 months, and 13 days since Jackie passed away. He was the light of my life, and I miss him as much today as I did when he left. I see couples today who fall in and out of love, like changing shoes. They have no idea what love is. It is not what you can do for each other, it is not what you have to offer each other in worldly treasures, but it is what you have to give from your heart — Love, unconditional love. That's the best gift you can ever give.

A Mother's Love

Don't look at my body as it gets old,
Look in my eyes so that you will know.
These are the eyes that first looked at you,
And loved you all through life as you grew.

A mother's love will never change,
But her body won't be the same.
As we grow older, we already know,
It is you who next to our place will go.

We cannot stay young; I wish we could.
But it is our love for you to be understood.
I love you forever, child of mine.
Don't be so sad when I have to leave you behind.

It's not your time, only mine...
For You know, I would never willingly leave you behind.

I Never Want You to Be Alone

I called you today just for a little talk.

You were too busy, so I went for a walk.

I took a walk down memory lane,

Wishing we were all young again.

What can I do? What can I say?

You never seem to have time on any day.

I'm too busy, my job is hectic,

I hope you never feel so neglected.

No one cares, and no one comes,
So, when I die, don't dare run.
You had a chance when I was here.
To spend some time but have no fear.

Although I'm gone from my Earthly home,
I will never be alone.
I have a heavenly family with arms open wide,
And smiling angels by my side.

Alone

It is exhausting to be alone.
When so many are already gone.
I'm alone, my heart is broken.
No truer words have I ever spoken.

Your life ended, and though my heart may beat,
There is not a moment that my mind doesn't want to retreat.
Back it goes to moments of days gone by,
When you were here right by my side.

The World continues as if life is normal,
But my heart is always mournful.
How do I forget that you're not here?
Sometimes, I even look for you to appear.

I know you have gone to your heavenly home,
But that doesn't help, I'm still alone.
You can't come back, and I can't go.
I continue to wait for that heavenly glow.

I have my family, and they are all great,
But sometimes it's hard to communicate.
They love and miss you too.
So please help me not to be blue,
Help me face tomorrow without you.
I loved you then, I love you now.
I'll always love you, this I vow.

From Graduation to Marriage

You were home on leave from the US Army, and I was getting ready to graduate from high school. We had corresponded by mail and now you were coming home in time for my graduation. I was so nervous; we had only been on a few dates, but I had known you all of my life. I didn't know if you were there, but you told me you would be… and I believed you.

It was over, and now, with my diploma in hand, I looked everywhere for you. I feared the worst; you were not here. I stood on the steps as tears rolled down my eyes. You didn't come. As this flashed across my mind, I heard your voice, "Are you looking for somebody?" That's all it took!

We got married a few days later, on June 7, 1963. Our love was easy to see for all of our life. So, this poem is for you from your loving wife.

Tall and handsome, easy on the eyes.
You were a blessing in disguise.
You found me in a large crowd of white hats and gowns.
Home from the Army, all muscles, no frowns.
There was no way I tried to say.
We can't get married, and then you go away.

I loved you, and you loved me,
We went to my house on Church Street,
Told Mom we were getting married tomorrow,
She loved you, too, so there was no sorrow.
We went to Georgia the next day, filled out papers galore.
Did them all until there were no more.

We were married for Forty-nine years.

Three children, eight grandchildren, and eight greats!

16 reasons to celebrate.

Wish you were here!

Isaac Mathew III

Isaac, our firstborn, a beautiful boy,

He filled our lives with so much joy.

He was a smiling, happy child.

A heart of love so tender and mild.

He would give his toys to kids who didn't have any.

Just to see them smile without even a penny.

He grew so fast from elementary to High,

There, he learned his plans to apply.

He found his true love, Cheryl, and walked down the aisle.

Pledging his lover forever to stay by her side.

Jenny was born, a beautiful girl,

Around her finger, we were all twirled.

Yes, we spoiled her a little, maybe a lot.

She grew so fast, I forgot.

Ian was born a few years after.

What a smile he had,

always full of laughter.

Babies grow too fast and now they are grown.

Jenny and Ricky have Zoe and Olive, two of their own.

Ian will marry Taylor soon, a beautiful bride.

Soon to be always by his side.

Isaac, the quiet one, is now a granddad.

Makes me feel old, but I'm not sad.

Isaac, Cheryl, Jenny, Ricky, Zoey, Olive, Ian and Taylor,

All joined together to make this family even greater.

Daphne Dawn Wise

Isaac was two when Daphne was born.
Soon, around her finger, her Daddy was worn.
She had him from the first breath she took.
All she had to do was give him that look.

Curly hair and a pretty little face,
He wanted her dressed in satin and lace.
Years passed by, our little girl grow,
And she was beautiful from head to toe

Years pass by like they always do,
And she grew up and got married too.
Her first son was soon to be born
And much to our surprise, he no longer was one, but two.

With only weeks to spare,
We began to prepare.
Buy another one of everything!
Listen for those bells to ring.

Happy were we, our first grandchild had turned into two.
Joshua and Jesse were never blue.
They had each other, but that wasn't all,
They later had a brother, Sam, and he's tall!

Jarrett Jason Wise

Jason was our baby the last to arrive.

Our house turned into a beehive.

Our family of two turns from 3 to 4, and now 5.

I'm surprised to still be alive.

We had fun as our children grew.

There was nothing for them that we would not do.

Jason is married and he and Tina have two.

Kristopher and Cassie, he's a Marine she's Navy blue.

I must admit, Jason may have been spoiled

But he was the baby and was not to be ignored

Our family went from 2 to 5 to 12 and now 18.

They are the best of everything!

Dickies

Lessons Learned

Happiness Is What You Make It!

I read a quote that has really stuck with me. It isn't known or listed who made this particular quote but it is; "Just remember there is someone out there who is more than happy with less than you have." I have often said that happiness is what you make it. In order to make it, you have to be happy with what you have. Now, today, I am thinking, would I be happy with less than I have? I hope so.

I have thought about my mother a lot since she passed away. She lived a long life and was 102 when she passed away. I was told, "Well, you had her a long time." Yes, I did, but it didn't mean I wanted her to go, and I believe that made it even harder to lose her even though we knew she was ready.

I believe I can honestly say that when I was growing up, my mom & dad were happy. We didn't have much but I don't remember ever hearing mom and dad argue. Dad was a logger and he worked from early in the morning until late. He came home tired but was glad to be home. They always made sure we had food and clothes but there were no frills and extras. I never heard either of them complain about things we didn't have or things they wanted. Times were hard and things in our house were scarce. There were no extras in the pantry or closets but there was laughter and tears that were shed together.

Dad would always tell Mom on Sundays..not that she needed to be told, "Better cook today, you never know who is coming." That was oh so true. There were 11 of us and whenever we could we always went home for Sunday dinner. Guests were always welcome. Happy times and no one was looking for a table to sit down. The children sat on the floor and everyone sat where ever there was a place. No fancy dining room, no crystal chandelier or fancy dishes but food and a real plate (No, they probably didn't match but you know what, I don't remember, so why does it matter now?).

I remember my girlfriends coming home with me after school and sometimes spending the night. They tell me now how much they loved to come there because we had so much fun (no TV, no video games), so much food and they always felt welcome. Thinking back, I guess we did have a lot of food, but it was typically the same: some form of beans, potatoes, and cornbread. Our church group would have cookouts and parties in our backyard. This was not due to our large manicured lawn, but because we lived on Church Street where it dead-ended at the railroad tracks. Behind our house was the Duval Street Viaduct, and Maxwell House Coffee was in view and in our nostrils. All the time. The fact was we did have a fairly large backyard, full of clothe lines but we knew when to duck if we were running.

At that time, you could buy a Nehi and Payday candy bar for 5 cents. We never had 5 cents unless we found some cold drink bottles and sold them. If we saw a penny back then, it had value, and we picked it up. Today, we just don't even bother to bend over to pick them up. Times have changed, monetary values have changed (not to mention today's moral values) and I have changed but some lessons I learned then are still with me today:

1. Trust God.
2. Life is precious and way too short.

3. There is nothing you will have in life more precious than the time you have today with your family.
4. Be content with what you have but don't give up on your goals.

These are just a few of the things I learned. I will share more with you one day, but now I have to go to work. Thank you for allowing me to express my thoughts and I leave you with this final one for today from Philippians 4:11 Not that I speak in respect of want: for I have learned, in whatsoever state I am, therewith to be content.[12] I know both how to be abased, and I know how to abound: everywhere and in all things I am instructed both to be full and to be hungry, both to abound and to suffer need.[13] I can do all things through Christ which strengthened me.

This beautiful poem "If I Knew" was written by Sidney W. Johnston.

I found this poem a few years ago and the words reminded me to take the time today for things that we should do, because one day our tomorrow will not come.

If I knew it would be the last time that I'd see you fall asleep,

I would tuck you in more tightly and pray to the Lord, your soul to keep.

If I knew it was the last time that I would see you walk out the door,

I would give you a hug and a kiss, then call you back for one more.

If I knew it would be the last time, I'd hear your voice lifted in praise,

I would videotape each action and word, so I could play them back day after day.

If I knew it would be the last time, I could spare an extra minute or two,

to stop and say "I love you" instead of assuming you would know I do.

If I knew it would be the last time, I would be there to share your day, well,

I am sure you'll have so many more, so I can let just this one slip away.

Surely, there is always tomorrow to make up for an oversight,

And we always get a second chance to make everything right.

There will always be another day to say, "I love you."

and certainly, there is another chance to say, "Anything I can do?"

But just in case I might be wrong, and today is all I get,

I would like to say how much I love you, and I hope we never forget,

Tomorrow is not promised to anyone, young or old alike,

And today may be the last chance you get to hold your loved one tight.

So, if you are waiting for tomorrow, why not do it today?

For if tomorrow never comes, you will surely regret the day.

When you did not take that extra time for a smile, a hug, or a kiss.

When you were too busy to grant someone what will turn out to be their one last wish.

Hold your loved ones close today, whisper in their ear,

And tell them how much you love them and that you will always hold them dear.

Take the time to say, "I'm sorry," "Please forgive me," "Thank you," or "It's okay."

And if tomorrow never comes, you will have no regrets about today.

Our G.I.R.L.S. Group

This was written several years ago.

I spent the past weekend with eight of my very dear friends. We graduated from Andrew Jackson High School in Jacksonville, Florida. We had the opportunity to stay at Chateau Elan in Brazelton, GA. While we were there, we had a little bit of snow. It was cold, but it was beautiful. The Hotel & Staff were Four stars and more. Thank you, Chateau Elan, for an amazingly impressive weekend. The room, the food, and everything there was wonderful.

This time, while we were all together, I received a call about my son, Jason, who is a diabetic. His daughter, Cassie, was not able to wake him, and she had to call rescue. I received a call from Tina, his wife, that he was unconscious and unresponsive. While

I stepped into the hall to talk on the phone, frantically trying to book a flight home, I found out that the G.I.R.L.S. had immediately held hands and began to pray for him. When I came back into the room to update them, they told me they had already prayed, but if I wanted to, we would pray again, so they did. God answers prayers and He answered ours that day. In what seemed like hours, but was only a few minutes, I received a call, and they told me he was ok and had awakened with IV-glucose and was weak but was now doing good. Thank God his daughter was home at the time, and Rescue was able to revive him. God is still in control and guiding our lives.

We prayed again and thanked God for answering our prayers! Each event in our lives when we are together tends to tighten the bond that holds us together. There were nine females, nine personalities, and nine decisions every time we turned around.

We all know that nine females cannot be together without a few little attitudes or words, but this group of nine females allow that bond to make us stronger, and we forget those times and go forward. We do not leave without attitude adjustments that bring us all together again! These women are incredibly special in my life, and I want to say Thank you, G.I.R.L.S. for your love, prayers, and support. You have been with me through times of sorrow and pain but also in happy, good, fun times as well. I love you all and appreciate your love and support. Thank you for your prayers. We are truly blessed to have such friendship & love for each other after all these years. I look forward to our next G.I.R.L.S. trip."

G.I.R.L.S. stands for Girls In Real Life Situations because any time we are together we share our real-life situations, pray about them, and make sure we are all doing ok.

We spend time together, sometimes just a day.

Sometimes a week if we can get away.

One of our trips was to Boston by train.

What a great time, even in the rain.

We flew from Boston to New York City.

The view and the lights were all so pretty.

We took in all the sights and walked for miles.

Then we flew home with happy smiles.

Our group is not small and is open to all.

If you're a 1963 graduate give us a call.

No matter the size, we travel together.

We prefer sunshine but don't worry about the weather.

To Patt, Charly, and Bubbles, thank you all.

In my sight, you all stand tall.

You've been by my side in sickness and death.

I'm thankful for you, and all the rest.

For Sudharshan's Dog

I was talking to Sudharshan on the phone one day, and I told him I was working on a book of poems. He asked me how I wrote poems. I told him if I had the first sentence, I could easily write a poem. So, he says, "If I give you a sentence, can you write a poem?" "Yes, usually, I can." So, he gave me a sentence about his dog at his feet while he was eating ice cream. "Ok," I said, "I will call you back in five minutes." Here it is:

I took out a bowl of ice cream and started to eat.
Then I heard a noise right at my feet.
A pair of big eyes the color of brown,
were looking at me with a large frown.

A bowl of ice cream, I said with a grin.
You can't eat this stuff, my little friend.
It will make you sick, and I will be sad.
For you are the best friend I ever had.

Here's a doggy treat for you.
Now chew, and don't be blue.
Sherry and I are here, right by your side.
If you are good, we will go for a ride.

Host Users' Group

I served on the Springer Miller Host Users' Group for many years. I enjoyed my time there and became friends with so many people. I hated to leave it, but I finally had to give it up and retire. They were some of the best years of my life, and I learned so much.

I went to the Host Users' Group for the very first time.
Wow, I was impressed, our stars aligned.
The people were friendly, we were all the same.
Working in hospitality, learning how to improve our game.

The sessions were endless, they covered each job.
Front Desk, Reservations, Accounting, we all had a choice.

Attend what you need and let them know if we need more.
Then someone asked, would you like to run for the Board?

This is my first conference, I said with a grin.
I would not know where to begin.
You're a great fit because you can't be ignored.
We've watched you, so yes, run for the board.

So, I ran without approval from work.
I felt it was a duty that I couldn't shirk.
Never expecting to win, I knew no one,
But I did and oh, what a run.
We hold a conference in November each year.
These are the memories I will always hold dear.
We made new friends and we worked hard,
The conference grew larger and now it is better by far.

So, if you are a Springer Miller user and do not attend,
Listen to me, my Hospitality Friend.
Go and learn this coming November,
It is a conference you need and will always remember!

If Tomorrow Never Comes

"If Tomorrow Never Comes" is a song by American country music artist Garth Brooks. I love this song, but I have written a version for those of us who have loved ones whose tomorrow didn't come.

Our worldly possessions are not the most important things as we live and look back on our lives, but the greatest possessions we can have are the precious memories created by taking the time and never being too busy for our family. Will they realize how much you love them if tomorrow doesn't come? I can assure you that our children, grandchildren, and one of our great-grandchildren knew how much he loved them. I also guarantee that they still feel his hugs after all these years. I know because I can. Love is the greatest gift that one generation can pass on to the next. Make sure you accomplish it today, for tomorrow will not arrive.

If tomorrow never comes, well, it does come and when it does, it's heartbreaking and life-shattering. But you can answer like I did. I knew how much he loved me when his tomorrow didn't come!

His Tomorrow Didn't Come

Sometimes, late at night, I would lie awake, and he would not be sleeping. Cancer gave no peaceful sleep as he lay there in the dark. When I turned on the light and saw the pain on his face, the thought crossed my mind: If he didn't wake up in the morning, I would never doubt the way he feels about me in his heart.

His tomorrow didn't come,
But I knew how much he loved me.
He tried in every way to show me every day.
That I was the only one
And when his time on earth was through
And I had to face this world without him,
The love he gave me in the past will be enough to last.
His tomorrow didn't come.

We've lost loved ones in our lives,
Who never knew how much we loved them.
And we live with the regret.
That our true feelings for them never were revealed.
So, we made a promise to ourselves.
To show our love in every way and avoid that circumstance.
Where there's no second chance to tell them how we feel.

His tomorrow didn't come.
But I know how much he loved me.
He tried in every way to show me every day.
That I was the only one
And when his time on earth was through
And I had to face this world without him.
The love I gave me in the past.
Will be enough to last.
His tomorrow didn't come.

So, tell that someone that you love.
Just what you're thinking of
If tomorrow never comes!

Forever Mine

Today is the day you will make Taylor your wife.
Remember your vows, she is yours for all your life.
Always love each other the way you do today,
Never give up or go astray.

Soon you will see her, all dressed in white.
She will have a glow like a bright shining light.
More beautiful today than any other,
Promising each other there will never be another.

As you stand and look down the aisle,
Across your face will be a big smile.
The love of your life
Today will become your wife.

May you always be as happy as you are today.
Remember the words you chose to say.
I love you forever until the end of time.
You will always be, Forever Mine.

For Ian and Taylor Wise

Prayer Changes Everything

I've prayed for certain things in life,
Health, BO, and a heart of love.
These prayers were answered, every one,
But only when I learned to pray, thy will be done.

Lift your prayers to God and let Him do the rest.
He needs not our help, only our trust.
Putting your faith in him, is truly a must.
I prayed for God to heal you, to take away your pain.

I didn't want to lose you, but my loss was Heaven's gain.
You left me here, with pain on your face,
But when I see you again, I will see your grace.
Through much pain and sorrow,
You left here with no tomorrow.

Your life here was spent, your days were gone.
You left me here all alone.
God's grace is sufficient, I've heard you say
So many times, even on our wedding day!

My loss is Heaven's gain,

Keep smiling, Sweetheart; I'll see you again!

Lesson Learned

A couple of years ago, it was a beautiful Saturday, and I decided I needed to pressure wash the house. It was a beautiful sunny morning, so I set about the task of moving everything off the porch. There were large, heavy flowerpots and porch furniture, but it was early, and I felt good, so I made it around the house, efficiently spraying off all the dirt, dust, and dead bugs.

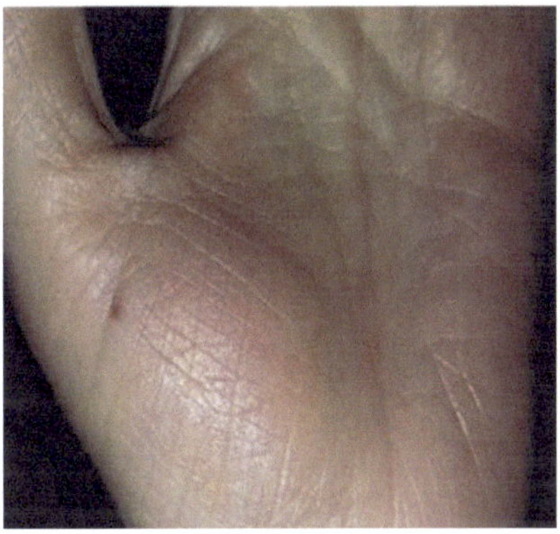

Wow, just a little more, and I will finish, but being the perfectionist that I was, I saw something on the white railing. I tried to remove it and pushed as hard as I could. I felt a sting and saw just a drop of blood, and my hand started hurting. I thought it must have bleach in it, so I went into the house and washed my hands. That didn't help; it was killing me, but I had to get all those plants back up on the porch. Finally, after I had dragged the last heavy flowerpot back up, I went inside and called Daphne, but she wasn't home.

I drove down the road to see Brad and Cindy. I thought I was a sissy because it hurt so bad. Brad told me I needed to get it checked that it had something in it. So, I said, "I'll go to urgent care."

"Nope," he said.

"You need to go to the emergency room."

I went back to the house, called Daphne, and told her I needed to go to the emergency room. Guess what?? It is Shrimp Fest Weekend, and impossible to get onto the island with all the traffic, so we went to Jacksonville. It was closer anyway. We signed in, sat down, and waited for 3 hrs!

Finally, I made it to the back. The exam was followed by x-rays, and by now, this little spot had my hand throbbing. I thought, "What a big sissy, you can barely see it." So, the doctor looked at the X-ray and finally came back to tell me that she could see that there was something in it, but she couldn't remove it because she couldn't see the angle at which it entered. So, she needed to do a sonogram, which hurt like crazy, but she still couldn't see the angle at which it entered the skin.

She called someone else in to do the sonogram so she could look at the wound while he did the sonogram. She finds the angle and is saying how she can cut it, and he tells her no, she can't. He tells her to look at it; it is in the muscle.

The doctor looks at me and tells me she has to call a surgeon. It is a splinter; for goodness' sake, take it out! Well, I guess I never do anything the easy way. The surgeon has already left since it is about 3 am, and now I will have to see him in his office on Monday.

Great, because I am ready to go home, but first, they need to immobilize my hand – No more using that muscle. The next thing I know, they are bringing in a cast cart to put a cast on my hand. I thought that was the most ridiculous thing I had ever heard. "A cast, it is just a splinter!"

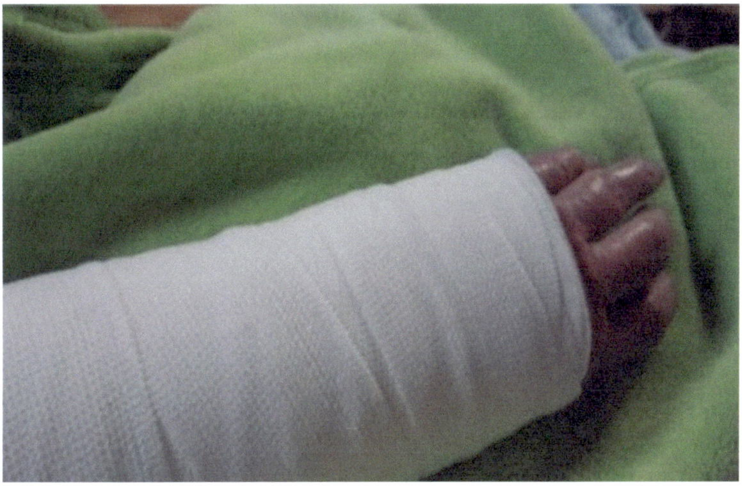

Saturday morning, and I tried to sleep in because my hand was killing me. It doesn't help when you are allergic to all NSAIDs, aspirin, Tylenol, etc.... All I had to do was make it one more day, and I would see the doctor on Monday.

Monday morning finally arrived, and what a beautiful day! Daphne and I were at the doctor's office early. I sat down while Daphne checked me in, and as they were looking for my appointment, Daphne was trying to explain that the hospital called him, and he told me to be here early so he could remove the splinter in his operating room. She told us to have a seat, and they would be with us shortly.

We waited patiently for the first hour, and the second hour, I was almost in tears, then finally, the receptionist looked up and saw me. Her face was priceless, and I knew she had forgotten me. Needless to say, she brought me to the back immediately, and I only had to wait a few minutes for the doctor. He smiled and apologized for the wait as he took off my cast.

"I am pretty sure we can remove this in our operating room. I will go look at your x-rays." Do you know that funny feeling that comes over you sometimes? Well, I had that feeling, and sure enough, when he came back, his words were, "I can't do that here; I need a hospital operating room!"

One more day to wait; my surgery would be tomorrow morning. I was put to sleep and awoke to the feeling of being intoxicated. The splinter was in the muscle, and each time I used it, it just pulled it in further. All over and down (down should be done) with, so I went home—no more pressure washing houses for me. Lesson learned.

Stop And Smell The Lemons!

Sometimes, when we have lemons and don't want lemonade, we just need to stop and smell the lemons!

Once upon a time (Oops, I forgot this is not a Fairy Tale but the absolute truth.), there lived a nice "older woman" in the small town of Yulee. Yulee – most people don't even know it exists - unless they are going to Amelia Island and see the sign on I-95 close to the Georgia line that says Amelia Island, Yulee, and Callahan. Now, I don't leave Yulee often, not that I am trapped here, and I do like to travel.

So, this is my lemon travel story (The smell of lemon is said to enhance your performance and attitude, sending you to a positive place). Let's see how positive this trip is!

I was looking forward to my trip to HITEC, which was taking place in June 2014 in Los Angeles. All packed and ready to go, I thought my flight was at 1:30, so I planned to leave at noon, which would give me thirty minutes to arrive at the airport and an hour to get through security and arrive at my gate. I was strolling through the airport by 12:30 and went quickly through security, thank you PRECHK! One gentleman was in a big hurry, so I let him get in front of me. His flight was leaving soon.

I made it through security and stopped to look up at the screens to find my gate. I found it, and then I found out that it was already boarding. No problem; it was quick to get to that gate, and I was even on time to board in my correct zone. The gentleman I had let go ahead of me was in the zone after me, a small world. Today is my Lucky Day. I have the PRECHK boarding pass, Zone A, and the flight was full, so I saved $25 by checking my luggage at the gate.

I was sitting on the plane, making small talk with my neighbor, when the engine started, but we didn't move. After several very long minutes, we finally started moving, but in the wrong direction. We are backing up when we hear that dreaded announcement. We are backing out more to keep the plane cooler until we take off, which was delayed due to storms in Atlanta.

Now, I don't know what it is about Atlanta, but there must be a problem with that magnetic pull that affects all planes within a 300-mile radius. After spending two hours on the sauna flight, we were told that our plane had some mechanical problems – I think we had already guessed that - and we would be deplaning. We need to go to the desk quickly, and they will book us on another flight.

You guessed it, the next leg of the journey is to run, rush and push all people out of the way because you know your flight is more important than anyone else. Finally, it was my turn to speak to the kind person at the counter. He told me he didn't have anything but would make a call to a "Fly the Friendly Skies" representative and see if they could get me on their flight to LA. *"Yes, they can. Go straight across (where that two-mile line is), and they will get you on a flight to Houston and then LA. Don't worry about your luggage; we will send it over."* Yes, it is definitely my lucky day. The stars are shining down on me. Awesome.

I go over to "Fly the Friendly Skies," and what a great deal they offer me, they can get me to Houston tonight and LA tomorrow morning by 9 AM. *"Oh, that won't work for you? Sorry, check back 'over there.' Oh, your luggage! No, we never got it. It is probably still 'over there.' You know how slow it is to get things done!"*

Now, I am standing in an even longer line 'over there' back where I started. They can also get me to LA by 9 AM tomorrow, but they will be glad to give me a room – My head actually rotated all the way around... A Room... I live fifteen minutes away, where I have a whole house. I do not need a room; I need a flight to LA. *"Sorry, that is the best we can do." Oh, yes, your luggage. Go down to baggage claim and see if it is there."* *Leave the secure area?* I *ask. – "Yes, you aren't going anywhere tonight."*

Frustrated, it is now 5 hours since my flight should have left – 30 minutes before I would have landed in LA, and I am in the luggage claim area, where everyone is great, looking for my luggage. They looked, the supervisor looked, and my luggage was nowhere to be found. *"Sorry, it could be here in Jax, or Atlanta, Houston, or LA."*

Called my boss to let her know I cannot leave until tomorrow morning. She told me to call the 800 number and ask for a supervisor. I told her it wouldn't do any good. I had checked with everyone already, and they had no flights. *"Oh, yes, they do. Call a supervisor."* So, I did, and after dropping my call four times after I had been on hold forever (my phone was on its last leg since I had been here all day; it was already doing its final beep-beep), I got a very nice supervisor who told me, *"Get back to the gate there is a plane boarding right now, and she would get me on it."*

Lesson learned here, always call the 800 number because they know more than the people who are at the airport desks (This only applies to airport service, not your cable provider)

Once again, I am strolling through the airport at a breakneck pace. I have no luggage, no ticket, and no current boarding pass (only the one I used earlier). I started to explain, but she sent me on through and said, you are fine. I made it by running to the plane, the last one on board, but finally made it to Atlanta, where our connecting flight was only delayed an hour!

Finally, I see the beautiful lights of LA. What an impressive sight tonight! We landed, and I thought since my luggage started early that morning, I would check just in case it had arrived ahead of me.

Have you ever been to LAX? I went down to the bowels of the airport only to find I had no luggage at Terminal 6 – However, they told me it might be at Terminal 7. Ok, that is not far. I'm at 6, and I need to go to 7, so how hard is that? Right next door, they said! Now, in Yulee, right next door, maybe a few hundred feet, and I am no sissy, so glancing around where there were several people asleep on the floor and sidewalk, I stepped outside.

Walking outside in the dark at 1 AM in LA by myself was an awesome experience, causing my heart to thump loudly and my feet to move quickly past all those doors -6-6-6-6-6-7A-7-7-7-7. Finally, one was open, and I went inside. Everyone in the luggage area was truly kind. I visited all the interior rooms full of luggage with them so that if it was there, I could easily recognize it. The rooms had every color, shape, and size of luggage - but not mine. So, they told me I had to return to Terminal 6 to file my missing luggage claim. Seriously? So, I went outside again past the sidewalk sleepers to -7-7-7-7-7-7A-6-6-6-6-6 and filled out my forms (All these doors with the same number? Yes, and they are not close together)

By now, I am really having fun! Time to take a Taxi and get to the hotel. I am tired and have been up since 5 AM, so with the three-hour time difference, I have been up for 24 hours. I waited for 30 minutes to catch a Taxi — a short ride — beautiful hotel, flawless check-in, and the staff was great! Did I need someone to help me with my luggage — no, I travel light!

With the key in hand, I got on the elevator, off at my floor, and went down a series of three twisting hallways. Finally, at last, my destination tonight; I am at the door to my room where a nice bath and soft bed are waiting. They were still waiting when my key did not work! I had to go back — yep, down three corridors to a phone by the elevator. They told me that someone would be right up, so I just needed to wait outside my room.

He arrives with a smile on his face, so kind and so patient. He inserts my key… just to see if I did not use it correctly, I guess. He said, *"No, it doesn't work for me either; let me try the master key."* Still smiling, his master key does not work either. He now must go back down three hallways and downstairs to get the machine to open the door. Ok, no problem, it is not his fault, so I am patient. I understand these things since I have worked in hospitality for many years at beach resorts where salt air plays havoc on locks.

He returns and has a radio, and someone will talk him through the task of opening the door with his little machine. Hey, I say, *"It's your lucky day. I can help you, and I have done this before at the hotels where I worked."*

"Oh no, he said, you are a guest."

I was thinking, yes, I am, but I know how to do that, and I am an exhausted guest. He was on his radio and calling,*"Come in seven,"* Finally, after many unsuccessful attempts explaining over the radio how the machine works, #7 came to the rescue and got the door open. Easy he says, and I gave him my best smile.

The door is unlocked, but they cannot get it to open. Finally, the two of them push with their shoulders and get it open. Guess what?? Inside this door, there are two other doors. They must use force with the inside door to open it as well. Once inside, we were greeted with the smell of something terrible. I am beyond tired, want a bath, and I am ready to go to bed. I am not a picky person, but I could not stay there.

My new-found friend called the front desk, *"The guest is not happy with the room."* Not happy, how about I cannot breathe in the room, not to mention that at the age of 69, my shoulder and arm bones might be a little fragile if I try to open the door with force and I am too fat to pick my heavy leg up and kick it open. They moved me to another room (Back down the three halls to the elevator and then rewinding two more corridors to the room where he was able to open the door with his master key). He was amiable and told me he would just slide my new keys under the door so that I could get some rest. The next day the other door was opened, and I had a beautiful suite.

The first airline had given me a bag that had a tee shirt and other necessities in it. Finally, my teeth were brushed, and I had a nice warm bath plus a clean tee shirt. What an awesome day!

I set my alarm so that I could sleep a couple of hours; then, I went to meet the others for breakfast in my clothes from the day before, and no makeup or hair spray. That was not a pretty sight with wrinkles in my clothes and lines two deep and four across on my face. My friend loaned me some makeup, and we went to the conference. I smiled as people passed by or stopped to see Datavision. It was another awesome day.

That afternoon we went shopping for some clothes since we had dinner with clients that evening and I think two days in the other ones had been enough. So, now, with new clothes and borrowed makeup, I felt like a new person. My luggage arrived later that evening while we were at dinner.

The rest is history. It was a fantastic trip. LA is beautiful, HITEC was great, sand our booth looked terrific. I saw old friends and made new ones.

In the grand scheme of life, these were all minor issues and made life "interesting for a day." No one was hurt, and no one died.

Sometimes, we just need to slow down and smell the lemons. *(I heard it would help you keep a positive attitude!)*

Just A Few Thoughts for You Today

To keep our sanity and survive today, we need to think about what is most important in our lives. Is it merely surviving today and making it through tomorrow, or is it doing our best today and looking forward to tomorrow? How you think and what you believe controls your attitude for today and tomorrow.

In other words, your attitude is determined by your altitude. What is your altitude today? Are you flying in low clouds, or are you soaring high above the clouds and basking in the sun? It's all up to you, so let's see where your altitude is today.

It was a rough time for all of us during the pandemic. It had not been easy for anyone, no traveling, visiting family, or work as we usually did. How well did we handle this situation of staying home and being inside? How did we do with Social Distancing?

I am alone most of the time unless I am traveling for work; and I am pretty much inside the house all the time or working in the yard. It wasn't that I had to, it was just that I had gotten into the habit of being comfortable staying at home.

Okay, since I am dictating to Siri, that word depression came out before I even thought about it. Now, that makes me think! If anyone asks me, I will say no. I'm not depressed, it's just lonely at home. So, it makes me wonder, what is the definition of depression? I found this online:

1. Persistent depression or feelings of sadness.

2. Self Loathing - doubting that you can do anything right, low self-esteem, and suicidal thoughts.

3. Loss of interest in all activities.

4. Irritability and isolation - challenging to be around and avoiding other people.

5. Anxiety - feeling that you will fail personally and professionally.

6. Loss of energy, poor concentration.

7. Disturbed sleep patterns - lethargic with a lack of hope.

8. Change in appetite and body weight.

9. Reckless behavior.

10. Suicidal Tendencies

Wow, what a list! Did you have any of these? I hope I'm not the only one, or I would be depressed. I was going to write something happy to lift us up during this time. It was not on my plan to write about depression, but I believe God lays certain things on our heart for a purpose. Maybe the reason is someone out there needs this, or perhaps I need to read it and say, I may have a few of these symptoms. I am sad, and I don't sleep well, but not all the time. I would say I am not depressed, so again our attitude can be determined by our altitude. It is time to soar back in those clouds and look at the sun. We have so much to be thankful for, and I am grateful for all the blessings I do have.

I am, however, familiar with depression and what it can do, so I don't speak about this lightly. I lost a sister to depression when she committed suicide. I know depression is real, and someone can have it and not know there is help available for you. If you think you have any of these symptoms or need to talk to someone, make that call. Depression can be just in sight. Call a friend and go to lunch or dinner. Life is worth living.

Smile, Have Fun, and remember a change of altitude requires a difference in your attitude. Soar with the eagles and enjoy the sunshine!

Hummingbirds

When I first moved into this house, I hung a hummingbird feeder and never saw any hummingbirds. This year, as I was picking up some mulch and potting soil, I saw a hummingbird feeder and decided to try it again. I didn't pay much attention to it, but I noticed that the food was going down. I cleaned it and refilled it, and much to my surprise, I finally saw one. Then I began to see it often – all morning long. It is only one. I am like

Alexa — I don't always know the answer, so I just enjoy seeing them as they come and go.

Today, it has been a beehive of activity there, so I raised my blind and placed my phone on the window frame. Wouldn't you know it rang just as those little wings were fluttering, just about ready to start drinking that delicious, sweet nectar! Not to be deterred, one returned shortly, and I took some pictures. As I was marveling over the wings beating so fast and the long beak, I thought about how plain this little bird of mine is. Where are all those beautiful colors you see in all the pictures?

Then I thought about what I had read about hummingbirds: They have the smallest bodies and the largest heart, which beats up to 1,260 beats per minute; they have the largest breast and flight muscles in proportion to body size of all birds. They also have the largest brain and are the only living bird that can fly backward and forward, up and down, sideways, or just hover in one spot. However, with all these unique and awesome features, they have weak feet and only use them for perching.

Hummingbirds have an extremely high metabolism and therefore require a lot of food. I read once that all birds in relation to size eat more than an elephant. It is definitely so with these. I guess that is why their wings beat so fast—they have to move a lot to find all that food every day! I don't need the beautiful colors to enjoy these little birds, although I am sure they would be beautiful. They are unique and fascinating, and that is enough for me. I'm thankful that God has blessed me with so much, particularly this or these little birds that come by to visit and enjoy the sweetness that is left out there for them. It is true that beauty is in the eye of the beholder. We just have to look for it!

Memories

A memory from 7 years ago when things were a lot different came up, and today, I see a lesson to share.

While I look at this picture, I realize now how bad Jackie looked. Seeing him every day, it didn't seem quite as bad, but now, looking back, I know.

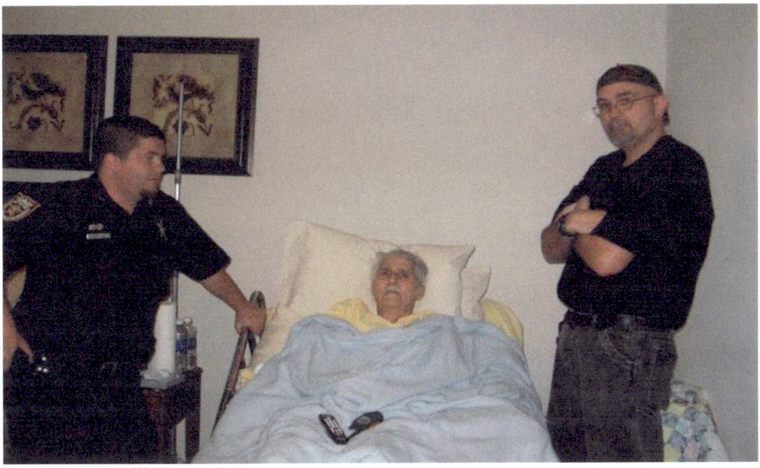

Here, in this picture, what I see is Jackie fighting to live. His right lung was removed, chemo and another simple surgery in his sinuses were done. It is where we almost lost him due to a severed artery, which created a paralyzed vocal cord, and he also lost the ability to swallow. He was a fighter, but more importantly, he was an example to our children, Isaac, Daphne, and Jason, and our grandchildren Jesse, Joshua, Samuel, Jenny, Ian, Kristopher, and Cassie. Great Grandson, Trenton.

He did see one of our great-grandchildren, Trenton, who is now 15. Grandchildren, Kristopher is a US Marine; Cassie and Joshua are home after serving in the US Navy. Jesse is a Police Officer. Sam is a mechanic. Jenny is married to Ricky Cumberland, and they have two girls, Zoey and Olive. Ian was recently married to Taylor, and you probably read their poem and saw their picture earlier.

We now have 7 greats…Zoey, Olive, Parker, Trenton Easton, Zane, Haley.

I look at our pictures, and today as I look around, the house is different, and the furniture and décor are mostly the same. I see things we bought and shared together, but even more, I see pictures of a family that he always had time for. No matter what time it was, whether it was a phone call to ask Dad, (Papa Jack) a question, or a visit for advice, or just to talk, he was always there...

It's not possessions that are so important as we live and look back on our lives, but the precious memories created by taking time and never being too busy for family. If tomorrow never comes, will they know how much you love them? I can tell you without a doubt these children can, and I guarantee you they can still feel those hugs...even after all these years. I know because I can.

Love is the greatest gift one generation can leave to another. Make sure you are doing that today because one day, your tomorrow won't come.

. . .For when I am weak, then am I strong.

2 Corinthians 12:11

He's My Son

Sometimes in life, we meet someone,
Who makes an impression and is lots of fun.
I met someone several years ago…
How we became friends, I will never know.

He is always smiling, working, but having fun.
Soon, he became more like a son.
He came to install Datavision in our office.
Then he trained us, and the system was flawless.

He made our lives easier and our hours less.
The reporting before had always been a mess.
Now, it was automated and easy to do,
But how it worked, I don't have a clue.

Several years later, I lost my job.
He said that's ok, you've got a laptop.
Then he gave me a job working from home,
I believe my first trip was a visit to Rome.

I traveled, had fun, and learned a lot.
Slowed down from a run to a mild trot.
His name is Sudharshan, he's my son,
Always thoughtful, smiling and having fun.

Yes, he's like a son,
I love him dearly.
He Loves me too
I see that clearly.

I've Been Loved By The Best

What can I say? What can I do?
I will forever love only you!
Cancer came and you had to leave.
My heart forever will always grieve.

Life goes on, our children's families are now grown.
Great-grands are now all at home.
Eight grand and eight greats,
I wish you were here to celebrate.

I can't bring you back, nor do I wish to do so.
God said it was time for you to go.
We love you; we miss you, but we understand.
You had to go when He took your hand.

When the sun shines bright, we know it's you.
Smiling on us so we won't be blue.
Keep smiling on us as we wait our time.
God knows what is best down the line.

We didn't have a big, beautiful wedding or a fancy home, but we did have beautiful children, grandchildren, and great-grandchildren.

We had more than the average hospital stays, accidents, and illnesses. When he worked, it was for long hours; sometimes, I worked as many as three jobs at a time. It was our love and faith that kept us together through it all and God provided our every need!

It wasn't always perfect; life never is, and our faith grew as our love and happiness did! Happiness doesn't come because everything is going our way, it comes because we learned that God is in control and his way is perfectly planned for each one of us.

This could have been written as an introduction to my book! It describes perfectly our path in learning to live — One Day at a Time, which was written to encourage and inspire you to believe, trust God, and learn to live in the present. Yesterday is over and can't be changed, tomorrow isn't here yet, and whatever happens, we face it tomorrow!

Roses — From A Thorn To A Flower

Small and ugly little plant,
With thorns that bite but are loved by ants.
I fertilized, I watered, and waited for it to grow.
It was so very, very slow.

Winter came, and it withered to the ground.
Goodbye ugly flower, I'll see you around.
The sun came up, melting the snow,
Allowing the ugly plant to grow.

I passed by it once in a while.
It always brought me a big, happy smile.
Then, out of nowhere, the leaves came out.
Green leaves and thorns survived the snow and drought.

Red roses grew from buds to flowers.
It seemed to happen in just a few hours.
Butterflies 🦋 came to rest on the blooms,
Driving away all sorrows and gloom.

Cactus in Bloom

I watched the cactus as it grew,
As a small green plant, with no particular beauty.
Then, one day, it began to change,
A small bud appeared at the end, seemingly to grow out of duty.

A bud appeared on the end of each branch.
Small pink ones, all just the same.
They grew larger, and not just by chance.
Like a child, the bud began to grow,
Some grew fast, and some grew slow.

But each one beautiful in its own way,
And growing more beautiful every day.
Pink and red, flowers of many colors,
Just like children who love one another.

Each one different, yet the same.
Just like God made us to live, love, and grow in His Name.

My Mother

It's Monday, it comes every week.
Starting the week out with no time for sleep.
Go to bed early, I say with a grin.
That's the way it has always been.

Early to bed, early to rise.
No time here to compromise.
It's time to grow up from a child to a teen.
Get up early and get your room clean.

My mother taught me all through life,
Nothing is gained without hard work or strife.
Do your work first and play later,
There's nothing worse than a time waster.

As an adult, I now see clearly,
My mother loved me so very dearly.
These lessons I learned as she guided.
With love, she always provided.

I graduated with honors in school and in college.
I glance back now, so proud of this knowledge,
Knowing without her, I would be lost.
As a parent now, I see the cost.

It's not the money or things you can buy.
It's about the lessons you learned at her side.
She gave you her all, put her trust in God.
He gave her the wisdom to do a good job.

Mom

Mm, I remember your last birthday at 102.
You were so happy as we celebrated you.
On 100th, Dean made you a cake of 100 layers.
Over 100 people came, an answer to our prayers.

You and Dad raised us, all eleven.
Before you died, 7 of us were in heaven.
James, Joe, Gene, Bib, Johnnie, Mary, and Richard, 7 of 11.
These were the ones who left before you, the Seven.

You were so brave to carry on,
With most of your family already gone.
We had a party to celebrate you…
When you turned 102.

May 1, 2012, God took you home to rest.
Many people had good Mothers, but we had the best.
Now, since you left, Dean followed you.
It's been really hard, but we can't be blue.

I miss you, Dad, and all my sisters and brothers.

For a family like ours, there will never be another.

Jen

I have a true friend, her name is Jen.

But how and where do I begin?

She's like a daughter, with an Irish accent.

Our days together are always well spent.

We met through work several years ago.

A friendship, a kinship, laughter,

and fun.
She's like a daughter with an Irish
accent.
Her days together are always well
spent.
We watch her cook, and in the
kitchen she reins.
She's one of a kind and once you
meet her, you'll feel the same.
She's a hostess, like no other,
a friend who treats me like her
mother.

Poems of Love and Loss

Lessons Learned

Bonnie Shetters Wise

Poems of Love and Loss

Lessons Learned

Bonnie Shetters Wise

Made in the USA
Columbia, SC
07 October 2024

43641088R00067